Edith Costanza

Regrouping

After Job Loss

A Guide

I0035889

Edith Costanza, M.Ed.

Regrouping After Job Loss
Table of Contents

Edith Costanza , M.Ed.

Edith Costanza, M.Ed.

Work is love made visible.
-Kahlil Gibran

I want to speak to those of you who suddenly find yourself unemployed. It is heart stoppingly scary. You ask yourself: "How will I pay my mortgage, my bills, buy food, take care of my family?" There are absolutely no easy answers, and what we read in the newspaper and see on television just compounds the fear. On the one hand, we can see we are not alone, but on the other, we also notice that in spite of being told that things are getting better and the economy is improving, such might not be the case in our world or in the world of our friends.

Don't panic. This guide has grown out of my expertise working with two nationally known career continuation organizations. Most importantly, I have been in your situation, and have successfully regrouped after job loss.

What I hope to offer here are proven ways to find strength and encouragement as you make your way to what comes next. This is a working guide. You will begin by gathering your spiritual, emotional, intellectual, and physical resources. You will place yourself on a daily schedule that incorporates personal time and provides ways for you to stay refreshed and positive. You will structure and devote the time necessary to reflect upon your life. You will identify your own particular set of skills and qualities. You will see how these skills and qualities might transfer into similar work or morph into something new. You will use techniques such as brainstorming to jumpstart your job search as you explore alternative types of work and lifestyle. Finally, you will read about others who have walked this path before you and have successfully regrouped after job loss.

To gain the most benefits from this guide, I suggest you put yourself on a schedule, read through the entire guide before you begin working it, and immediately incorporate the suggestions offered under R2: Refill. I want you to find ways that will make you feel whole and worthwhile, because you are, and know without a doubt that you have much to contribute to the world. If you have a job but know a friend who just lost theirs, get this guide for your friend.

Edith Costanza, M.Ed.

Edith Costanza, M.Ed.

R1

Respond

Edith Costanza, M.Ed.

Edith Costanza, M.Ed.

R1: Respond

Consult not your fears but your hopes
and dreams.

Think not about your frustrations but
about your unfulfilled potential.

-Pope John XXIII

Edith Costanza, M.Ed.

Visit human resources to learn about your options

Human resources will provide you with answers to such questions as: "Will I be offered a severance package?" "What is the process if I take early retirement?" "How do I apply for unemployment?" "Will I be offered outplacement services?"

Rely on something greater than yourself

From what source do you receive the courage to keep going? This is the faith part, and I am not going to preach. We all rely on something: God, Mother Earth, history, conventional wisdom, past experience, science, the Universe, family, friends, and relatives. Anchor yourself to your source and absolutely know you will get through this time in your life.

Mobilize your family

If you have children tell them about what is going on regarding your family situation. You are smart and can couch it in a way where your child won't worry. Let them know that for a while, the whole family may need to cut back and do without extras. Ask for their help and offer them the opportunity to see what sorts of things they can do without for a while. Rework your budget so that your family can maximize what monies you have. Being a family means facing both good and challenging times. You are their example for how to handle life.

Take advantage of outplacement services

Most organizations offer outplacement services. Or, if not, most cities have career centers which offer services to people who are unemployed. There is much useful information to learn in these centers. Usually, a representative will start off speaking about the grief cycle. This helps people understand emotionally, what it is to face a huge loss...livelihood and lifestyle. The mood swings and emotions encountered are explained and coping skills are offered. Topics that are also covered include the latest job search techniques such as résumé writing, budgeting, networking, interviewing, following up, and negotiating. Designing a daily schedule for your path forward is a useful tool. If you find that using a computer is intimidating, go to the public library and take advantage of their free computer classes for beginners. Your career center might also offer computer classes. Many churches offer support groups for those who are facing unemployment. You are not alone.

Face your fear and go through it

Job loss is scary, particularly in the current economy. In facing this loss, and making yourself capable of regrouping, it is crucial not to mask your feelings with alcohol, drugs, food, shopping, fantasy, over exercising or any other activity you tend to use in order to escape and not "feel."

You need to remain clear and grounded so that you can think and be open to inspiration and creativity.

Edith Costanza, M.Ed.

R2

Refill

Edith Costanza, M.Ed.

R2: Refill

Silence is the best refreshment.

—Wynonna Judd

Edith Costanza, M.Ed.

Edith Costanza, M.Ed.

Be still

You will devote a great deal of focus to intro-spection, research and self-reflection. Your efforts need time to be absorbed and internally processed. Can you commit to being still? Begin sitting still daily for 5 minutes and simply observe all the thoughts that pass through your head. This is a way to begin meditating, but I am not trying to force this on you. My goal for you is simply to relax your mind. I like to be still for a little while in the morning and simply listen to the sounds outside. Birdsong, the flow of traffic, the patter of rain are all sounds that soothe and bring peace. I want you to have pockets of peace in your day.

If you are never still, those wonderful intuitive thoughts and ideas can't get through the busyness.

Take daily breaks

In "recovery" circles there is a saying about a human "being" rather than "doing." It is a reminder for people to feel and accept their worthiness just for who they are rather than what it is they have done and accomplished. This is totally opposite to the messages our culture gives us. We are taught to accomplish, to "be all that we can be," to "just do it." And those, on the one hand, are fine messages.

However, couched in these messages are judgments, so on the other hand, this is not so great. We are constantly in the process of judging ourselves and others. We look at people's outsides... their looks, possessions, net worth and achievement, and rate ourselves as falling short. But we don't know how these people feel on the inside, nor is it our business to know. Life is to be savored, and enjoyed. Job placement services will tell you that you have a new full time job and that is to find a new job.

I am telling you to balance your job search with life and enjoyment of the precious gift of the day. Get on a schedule, and give five hours every day to doing the work entailed in job searching. In those other three hours, reacquaint yourself with who you are and what you love. Go for a walk, get an ice cream cone, read an article, plant some flowers, have lunch with a friend (you can double dip and network), but start being kinder to yourself. Happiness is a byproduct of living fully. All work and no play are compulsive and unbalanced behaviors.

Count your blessings then make a gratitude painting

Are you able to notice all the wonder that surrounds you? I think most of us take so much for granted. Let us begin with our physicality.

Most likely we can see, hear, taste, touch and, in most cases, get around. We can think, plan, dream, and create. We are composed, literally, of dozens of skills and talents that we use to help ourselves and others. We live in a rich society, and even the poorest of us still have access to avenues of help. Go to an art store and buy a large canvas and some permanent markers. Everyday write five things you are grateful for on that canvas, and keep adding to it. Write over it when you fill it up...this will take a while...and get in the habit of continuing this through your lifetime. It does several things: Your attitude will improve, you will stay out of self-pity, and you will have visual proof of just how much there is to celebrate.

Volunteer

Remember how I spoke about a certain set amount of hours to spend on the job search? While waiting to hear back from job applications, I suggest you devote some of those excess hours to volunteering. Volunteering gets you out of yourself.

Edith Costanza , M.Ed.

It increases your self-worth, because you see that you are still needed and can contribute.

Job loss is usually a big blow to our self-esteem. Yes, people still want and need your services! Do this from a generous heart, but also be aware that your volunteerism can lead to work.

Laugh every day

Look for and find the funny. If you are the serious somber type, start a funny file of cartoons in the newspaper, or go to the library and check out a joke book, or watch funny movies, or just observe what people wear, how they move, how they sound. We are a hilarious species. You will feel better when you are able to laugh.

R3

Reflect

Edith Costanza , M.Ed.

Edith Costanza, M.Ed.

R3: Reflect

Learn how to be happy with what
you have while you pursue
all that you want.

-Jim Rohn

Edith Costanza, M.Ed.

By designing a daily schedule, you have now established a safe place for yourself, a foundation from which to do the work necessary to regroup and recover after job loss.

This work starts with reflection.

Make a list of what makes life meaningful to you. This is your first step. The reason for making this list, as I will illustrate in the next section, is that everything one knows how to do or loves to do or enjoys doing can potentially transfer into a job.

What Makes My Life Meaningful

1.   Relationships
2.   Flexible Schedule
3.   Travel
4.   Love of nature
5.   Pets
6.   Gardening
7.   Art
8.   Acting
9.   Reading
10.   Photography
11.   Writing

To explain how reflection can be a tool to recreate our vision of the future I will outline myself as an example. For me a meaningful life is first of all about relationships. I dearly love the people in my life, even when I might have struggles with them. I think everyone I know offers so much... talents, positive qualities, imagination, strength and endurance, intelligence and humor, and love.

Second, I need the freedom of making my own schedule. I am willing to give up the security of the traditional for the possibilities that lie in the adventure of the moment. In fact, I responsibly meet the expectations laid out in the jobs I take on, but it is my choice to not be locked in to just one work experience in any given week. For example, my week is always composed of Friday where I work as an art therapist, but I may work as a Ghost Tour Guide on Tuesday and Thursday evenings, and give a workshop on Wednesday to a group of people. As a professional actress, I may be called at any time during the week to audition. This type of juggling keeps me enthused and excited about the projects I take on.

Third, I love to travel. Traveling is so interesting because I get to take in new views which feed my artistic soul, but I also get to experience how other people "do" life. While we all bleed red under the skin, life is not the same for everyone. People have differing values, customs, foods, music, traditions, ways of making sense of the world, ways of worship, etc. Our planet is varied and fascinating, and I rejoice in my world citizenship.

Fourth, I have a love of nature, hiking, and camping. Being outdoors is something that consistently refreshes my spirit.

Fifth, I enjoy a variety of pets. My pets are my family members. Recently, both my dogs died and I am still grieving their loss.

Sixth, my garden provides beauty and a hobby.

Seventh, is art...seeing art, reading and learning about art, making art, having art shows, and overall appreciation of art in all its incarnations.

Eighth, is acting. I get to delve into different characters, and just for a short while, experience another kind of life. Acting dovetails with reading which gives me the same gift of "other," as well as the beauty of the words and the writing.

Ninth, there is reading. I am in love with the written word. I want the knowledge and experiences reading provides for me.

Edith Costanza, M.Ed.

Tenth, there is photography. I often use photographs to capture scenes for future paintings or as documentation or illustration for other works.

Finally, there is writing. I like to document trips with writing, sketches, and photographs. I like to write about a variety of topics or things I think or things I have learned.

Step two involves writing answers to some questions. The answers will help anchor you in the now, may help identify barriers you may need to overcome, and may point you in a direction you have not previously thought about and one in which you might want to go.

Here are questions to consider. The first question is about privilege and entitlement. Why is it that we think bad things shouldn't happen to us? How is it that we make ourselves exceptions? There are no exceptions. We merely have to turn on the news to witness all types of disasters; both natural and man-made. In the tragic flotsam and jetsam of broken lives, people still regroup and continue.

The second question examines your ideas about material wealth and possessions. How much do you need as opposed to what do you want? In terms of regrouping, you may have to let go of some of your possessions.

Edith Costanza, M.Ed.

You may have to rework how you spend your money and adjust to a new reality. You are not your home or your car or your work. How much of your identity, your ego, is bound up in symbols? If you choose to have less will this make you less of a person?

The next question concerns happiness. Are you happy, really? Do you know what makes you happy? These elements, whatever they might be, are your internal signposts that can guide you as you regroup.

Next, can you ask for help? Is this humiliating for you? Does it strike at your idea of independence and self-sufficiency? What is your attitude when you give help to others? There are so many ways to find help during this time of job loss, but you must be willing to ask for and take the help offered.

Can you view this occurrence of job loss as a respite? It is so rare in life, unless we become ill, that we get a "time out." Being out of work provides an opportunity. Do you regret not ever having enough time to...? Now, you have some. Do you still have dreams? What were your dreams? Have you/are you fulfilling them? Are you living your dream? Do you have new dreams? What have you always wanted to do?

Dreams are realities waiting to be born. Writing about these dreams may inspire you towards a different type of career.

R4

REFRAME

Edith Costanza, M.Ed.

R4: REFRAME

Don't limit yourself. Many people limit themselves to what they think they can do. You can go as far as your mind lets you.

What you believe you can achieve.

-Mary Kay Ash

Edith Costanza, M.Ed.

You are not a victim. For you to successfully regroup, reflecting upon and listing everything that makes life meaningful for you puts things in perspective. You have developed in life a set of skills and qualities that are transferable into either a job similar to what you had or that will be the bedrock for developing new kinds of work. They are the seeds holding potential job options that could replace an old career with a new one. It is useful to be able to explore a wide variety of work resulting from these skills and qualities. I define skills broadly in terms of what I can do, make, or create. I include intellectual and manual skills. Qualities I define to mean a wide range of personality traits.

Using the list I created from my reflections, I will break down the things that I love into skills and qualities and then explore what types of work might fit. I am presenting these ideas first as a chart. At the end I extrapolate upon this chart, if you are the type of person that likes more detail.

Edith Costanza, M.Ed.

A Meaningful Life	Skills	Qualities	Possible Jobs
RELATIONSHIPS	Ability to make friends, socialize, problem-solve, resolve conflict, outreach to others	Reliability, consistency, humor, playfulness, acceptance, forgiveness	Teacher, professional trainer, motivational speaker, life coach
FLEXIBLE SCHEDULE	Self-knowledge, self-direction, ability to meet deadlines, can work independently, time management	Faith, trust, reliability, consistency	Shift work, 24 hour operations, part-time work that involves driving, service work
TRAVEL	Ability to read a map, design an itinerary, research, budgeting, good sense of direction, computer skills	Appreciation for other ways of life, patience, curiosity, acceptance, a non-judgmental attitude	Travel and write articles about travels in newspapers, magazines, or blogs

Edith Costanza, M.Ed.

A Meaningful Life	Skills	Qualities	Possible Jobs
LOVE OF NATURE	First aid, orienteering, know how to set up/break down camp	Physical endurance, appreciation for nature, Commitment to preserving the natural environment, not being dependent on creature comforts	Guided hikes or tours, lead adventure courses like Outward Bound
GARDENING	Digging, planting, mulching, landscape design and plant research	Physical strength, patience, persistence, observation, not mind "getting dirty"	Landscaping, working in gardening departments such as Lowe's or Home Depot, lawn service
PETS	Pet maintenance including bathing, brushing, feeding and exercise	Patience, responsibility, enjoyment, and empathy	Pet sitting in your home or others,' open a do-it-yourself dog/cat wash, open a pet products shop, provide mobile bathing services, dog trainer

A Meaningful Life	Skills	Qualities	Possible Jobs
ART	Know a wide range of techniques, familiarity with the use of different mediums, computer skills	Enthusiasm, art appreciation, experimentation, creativity	Teach art, make art full time or on commission, own a cooperative art gallery, host art "salons", muralist
ACTING	Cold reading, script breakdown, character development, movement, voice pitch, elocution, timing, decision-making, stage performance vs. film performance	Perseverance, determination, teamwork, patience, good memory, ability to think on one's feet	Jobs in print, voiceover, commercials, short films, feature films, live theatre, storytelling, historic or entertainment guide
READING	Physical ability to see and/ or feel (maybe you read Braille)	Love of the spoken and written word, imagination	Proofreaders and editors in book publishing, but also for newspapers, manuscripts, newsletters or websites

Edith Costanza, M.Ed.

A Meaningful Life	Skills	Qualities	Possible Jobs
PHOTOGRAPHY	Develop an artistic eye, know how to frame a shot, operate photographic equipment, computer expertise in Photoshop and other computer based programs	Work independently, Physical stamina, meet deadlines, creativity	Government or journalistic photographer, Independent contractor
WRITING	Spelling, punctuation, organize thoughts, proficiencies in technical and creative writing, computer programs and research methodology	Meet a deadline, work under pressure, organization, imagination, self-discipline	Craigslist, writer for newspapers, blogs, magazines or books

Edith Costanza, M.Ed.

The following describes the chart in a more detailed way. As far as the people in my life, let me begin with relationships.

Relationships:

Skills include knowing how to make friends, socialize, problem-solve, resolve conflict, and outreach to others.

Qualities demonstrated are reliability, consistency, humor, playfulness, acceptance, and forgiveness. I cannot begin to list the seminars I have given that have to do in some way with relationships. Just a few that come to mind are: Dealing with Difficult People, Diversity Training, Communication, Stress Management, Problem-solving, Team Building, Facilitation, Coping with Grief and Loss, Career Continuation, etc. Yes, I am a professional trainer, but the question you might ask yourself is what could YOU teach?

Flexible Schedule:

Skills include flexibility, self-knowledge, self-direction, ability to meet deadlines, ability to work independently, and time management.

Edith Costanza, M.Ed.

Qualities are faith, trust, reliability, and consistency. Shift work, work in places that operate 24 hours such as copy shops (I once worked for two years from 11pm-7am on the weekends while I began my consulting business); part-time work (I worked for over a year teaching traffic school at night and on the weekends); work that involves driving such as bus drivers, taxi drivers, or couriers; or other types of service work that happens after usual business hours can be explored.

Travel:

Skills include the ability to read a map, designing an itinerary, research, budgeting, good sense of direction, and computer skills.

Qualities are appreciation for other ways of life, patience, curiosity, acceptance, and a non-judgmental attitude. People get paid to travel and write articles about their travels...newspapers, magazines and now blogs might be possibilities.

Love of Nature:

Skills are first aid, orienteering, and knowing how to set up and break down camp.

Qualities are physical endurance, appreciation for nature, commitment to preserving the natural environment, and not being dependent on "creature comforts." There are people who make their living taking people on guided hikes or lead adventure courses such as Outward Bound.

Gardening:

A gardener's *Skills* include digging, planting, mulching, landscape design, and plant research.

Qualities needed are physical strength, patience, persistence, observation, and not minding "getting dirty." Landscaping, working in the gardening departments at various home improvement or hardware stores, or simply hiring out as a gardener doing planting, pulling weeds, or going into lawn service are options.

Pets:

Skills used in pet care include pet maintenance such as bathing, brushing, feeding, and exercise. *Qualities* needed are patience, responsibility, enjoyment, and empathy. Pet sitting, either in your home, or staying in someone else's home and taking care of their pets when the owner is away is a good source of income. Pet care services such as mobile bathing services where a groomer or bather comes to a home and bathes and grooms the dog/cat in their van or trailer set-up is a possibility. I know of a woman who opened her own pet grooming shop specializing in do-it-yourself baths for dogs and cats at half of what it costs to have your dog bathed and groomed at a vet. Her business is so successful that she expanded the shop to include food and a variety of pet products. Dog training is also a viable job.

Art:

Skills an artist uses covers a wide range of techniques and familiarity with different mediums. Skills such as teaching, drawing, painting, sculpture and now familiarity with the various computer art programs are crucial.

Qualities developed might be enthusiasm, art appreciation, experimentation, and creativity. Many people teach art as well as make art. Craft stores and fine art stores offer classes. There are people who own art galleries cooperatively, host "salons," have art crawls, make live art or performance art, paint murals for businesses or non-profits, and commission work from private clients.

Acting:

Skills begin with mastering cold reading and script breakdown then proceed to character development, movement, voice pitch, elocution, and timing. Decision-making is also crucial depending upon whether the role is dramatic or comedic, and whether the performance is for stage or film.

Qualities such as perseverance, determination, teamwork, patience, a good memory, and the ability to think on one's feet are also a plus. I have been acting professionally for sixteen years and audition for acting jobs in music videos, short films, commercials, and voiceovers. However, I recently began giving Ghost Tours which is a live storytelling venue. I get an hourly rate and tips. There are professional theatre companies which also pay their actors.

Reading:

Skills would be the ability to see and/or feel (perhaps you can read Braille), plus being able to read quickly.

Qualities are a love of the spoken word and imagi-nation. There is still a need for proofreaders not only in the publishing world, but throughout any business. Think of the person who proofreads manuscripts, newsletters, or websites.

Edith Costanza , M.Ed.

Photography:

Technology has changed this profession, but someone still needs to shoot pictures or document events.

Skills include the traditional ones such as developing an artistic eye, knowing how to frame a shot, and being expert with your equipment. Computer expertise with Photoshop and other types of technical editing is crucial, because images are now digital.

Qualities like being able to work independently, physical stamina, meeting deadlines, and creativity are all part of the package. Think about documenting any type of celebration or party, look at taking head-shots (actors always need headshots), or explore the traditional route of government or journalistic photography.

Writing:

Skills used are spelling and punctuation, the ability to organize thoughts in a clear and interesting manner, and a proficiency in different types of writing such as technical writing versus creative writing.

One also needs to be familiar with various computer programs and research methodology.

Edith Costanza, M.Ed.

Qualities needed are the ability to meet a deadline, the ability to work under pressure, organization, imagination, and self-discipline.

I have noticed on Craigslist many advertisements for writers, particularly those familiar with social networking. Of course there are the traditional routes of writing books or writing articles for magazines.

Edith Costanza , M.Ed.

R5

Reality Check

Edith Costanza, M.Ed.

Edith Costanza, M.Ed.

R5: **Reality Check**

Never continue in a job you don't enjoy
If you're happy in what you're doing
you'll like yourself.
You'll have inner peace.

And if you have that along with
physical health, you will have had more
success than you could possibly have imagined.

-Johnny Carson

In order to ensure a balanced view of ourselves, we now give some thought to things we don't like to do, or things that we don't do well.

Weaknesses

It is a reality that we all have weaknesses. During the regrouping process we examine our strengths, our likes, and use them as positive indicators towards certain types of work. The same can be said of our weaknesses and dislikes.

One of my dislikes is spending a lot of time on the phone. I absolutely hate making phone calls, maneuvering through electronic recordings, getting voicemail, and being put on hold. A job that would entail spending a lot of time on the phone would not be a good choice for me.

A weakness of mine is selfishness. I live alone so I am very used to having "my space and my time." While I daily make conscious choices to do things for others, it is challenging for me to give away or sell "my time." Last year I agreed to take a job two mornings a week as a caregiver to a woman currently experiencing health challenges.

The pay was great and the husband and wife are lovely people. The woman was and is a great model for me of both faith and acceptance.

I lasted one year. And then I noticed that I was just dreading going to that work. I felt hemmed in and claustrophobic and very sad. I quit.

In analyzing my decision, this is what I came to understand about myself. I have Crohn's disease and almost died about nine years ago. I feel I cannot choose to engage in any activity that I can't enter into happily and wholeheartedly because I do not know when I may "flare" and become very ill again. My client was reminding me too much of my own potential vulnerability and the possibility I might find myself immobile. This was/is distressing for me.

My philosophy is that I want to live my life as fully as I can during the time I have. I know now that work as a private caregiver is not the job for me no matter how great the pay or accommodating the client. Not everyone will have this response to that type of position. A friend of mine, whose father was ill, had caregivers who loved the work and were personally suited for it.

Another weakness of mine is gossip. I work one day a week at a particular non-profit organization. Because I am only there that one day, I do not allow myself to become involved either in gossip or office politics. This is very helpful. I can remain on good terms with ALL of my co-workers, and I am more productive because I am not wasting time agonizing about what I dislike about a particular person or policy.

Realistically acknowledging my dislikes and weaknesses is crucial since they can point me away from potential errors in choosing certain specific types of work.

Edith Costanza, M.Ed.

Edith Costanza, M.Ed.

R6

RE-IMAGINE

Edith Costanza, M.Ed.

R6: Re-imagine

Those people who develop the ability
to continuously acquire new and better
forms of knowledge that they can apply
to their work and to their lives will be the
movers and shakers in our society for the
indefinite future.

-Confucius

Edith Costanza, M.Ed.

Designing alternatives and finding gaps

Here is the exciting part. From my outplacement work, I learned that service work of some kind would be the fastest growing occupation, and in graduate school I was encouraged to look for "gaps." My definition of gaps are those undiscovered ideas that can yield new careers. I will warn you ahead of time that I hope to go as far "outside the box" as I can in terms of my thinking, and I encourage you to do the same.

But first, learn how to brainstorm

Do you know how to brainstorm, really? Let's review. I suggest getting with about five friends whom you perceive, without a doubt, are on your side and want the best for you. Get a flipchart and some markers and ask these several overhead questions, *one at a time*.

Question 1: What am I good at? Then have them respond to this question for five minutes while you write down their answers.

Do not talk, critique or stop their flow. Just record verbatim what they say

The result is you get an objective look at what others perceive as your skills.

Edith Costanza, M.Ed.

Question 2: What kinds of jobs could you see me doing? Go through the same five minute process, without stopping, and record verbatim. The result may yield some job ideas you have not considered.

Question 3: What sorts of jobs might we invent for me? Use the same process. Hopefully, you will glean some new and creative ideas.

Research

We now come to the last part of job explora-tion which is researching printed and electronic sources. Many of you may prefer researching on line, and if you took advantage of the career contin-uation option, you will have many search engines to visit. However, I like physically going to the library, since it is within walking distance from my home.

At the library browse the reference section. There are books that might spur you on, as to what types of occupations already exist. Here are some sources: ***The Big Book of Jobs*** by McGraw-Hill and the U.S. Department of Labor, and all of the ***Jist Works*** books by Michael Farr. Titles such as ***100 Fastest Growing Careers***, ***100 Careers Without a 4 Year Degree***, and ***Best Jobs for the 21st Century*** are some of his titles.

For sheer amusement, find **Odd Jobs** by Nancy Rica Schiff. Some of the jobs, not to mention the photos, might tickle your fancy and will surely bring a big smile, if not a huge guffaw! I think these are really excellent sources. I also recommend Dave Ramsey's book **EntreLeadership**.

Beware of overloading and getting overwhelmed

If you have taken the suggestions I gave earlier, and worked through the brainstorming, you will have intuitively found your focus. Basically, I want you to understand the true limitlessness of possible types of work and I want you to see that information in black and white.

Examples of alternative occupations that fill a gap

Here are some examples of what people have discovered and turned into livelihoods. What I noticed as I began thinking for this section is literally the hundreds of jobs having to do with your home, your property, your pets and/or your personal vehicle. I already mentioned the lady that started the do-it-yourself dog bathing service.

I also recently heard of a service that when you move, will come to your home, unpack your boxes and set up and decorate your new home.

The best question to explore is what do-it-yourself services might be unique and become your special business? Did you ever hear about the successful college students that started a dog poop scooping and disposal service? I know of a woman who has a successful concierge business. She takes care of the mundane tasks that her high powered clients do not have time for. She is the person who does their grocery shopping, picks up dry cleaning, schedules travel, etc.

Here are some everyday tasks that might morph into a business: housecleaning, grocery shopping, catering, preparing healthy organic dinners, give Mom and Dad a Break, a business where you take care of the kids and the household while the parents get a weekend to themselves, a house sitting service (live in someone's home as a caretaker if they have multiple homes), car maintenance services where you come to people's home and change the oil or engage in light mechanical repairs, or deliver and pick-up their car to be serviced and include driving them to work and/or picking them up from work, driving services for large organizations where employees travel a lot or for car dealerships, all the skills it takes to build a home, painting and decorating the home, etc.

Edith Costanza, M.Ed.

I am certain there is some sort of need associated with the home environment that has not yet been developed. For example, think about the relatively new job of ductwork cleaning.

Home Entertainment Jobs

I know of a woman who makes her living bringing her daiquiri machine to parties and serves frozen daiquiris to guests. I know of a woman who thought about (but as yet has not followed through) starting a business making Halloween costumes for children. There are lots of people who entertain at children's parties with balloon animals, or character appearances such as clowns. You also have the singing/stripping telegram businesses. Question: What types of home entertainment would you be willing to pay for? Do you have the skills or the inclination to do this type of work?

Edith Costanza, M.Ed.

R7

RE·EDUCATE

Edith Costanza, M.Ed.

Edith Costanza, M.Ed.

R7: Re-educate

Don't let the fear of the time it will take to accomplish something stand in the way of your doing it. The time will pass anyway; we might just as well put that passing time to the best possible use.

-Earl Nightingale

Edith Costanza, M.Ed.

This may be the point, where you decide to follow a new career path that will require re-education. If that is the case, then it is time to make an appointment with whichever institution you have chosen, and start orienting yourself to their enrollment and perhaps, financial aid processes.

Edith Costanza, M.Ed.

R8

Reconfigure

Edith Costanza, M.Ed.

Edith Costanza, M.Ed.

R8: Reconfigure

Our real problem is not our strength today;
it is rather the vital neccesity of action
today to ensure our strength tomorrow.

-Calvin Coolidge

Edith Costanza, M.td.

Edith Costanza, M.Ed.

Consider alternative lifestyles

There are exciting movements springing up all around the country. One trend I have noticed is how many charter schools are being established as well as how many people are home schooling. I do not necessarily agree with these ideas, but I think they are viable alternatives and hopefully, meet the unmet needs of the establishers. If this is happening in regard to education, it can also happen in terms of living arrangements.

There are communities being established that revolve around the idea of "intentional living." People are buying land and building housing because they and their friends want to dedicate themselves to a specific way of life. Again, I don't necessarily agree, but the creativity shown is what I am hoping you will tap into.

Suppose someone has a huge home that they might be in danger of losing, for example. What if they meet with an architect and have the space redesigned to accommodate three or four families, where each family has a private living area and shares a communal kitchen? This is a take on the old boarding house idea, and might prove a way to keep afloat for the owner as well as the other families willing to rent (or own) space. In America, we are so used to being "independent" that we forget that most parts of the world have a more cooperative approach to life.

Edith Costanza, M.Ed.

Edith Costanza, M.Ed.

R9

Regroup

Edith Costanza, M.Ed.

Edith Costanza, M.Ed.

R9: Regroup

*Far and away the best prize that life has
to offer is the chance to work hard
at work worth doing.*

-Theodore Roosevelt

Edith Costanza, M.Ed.

Keep hope alive - some stories.

This next section is a collection of stories about people who have regrouped. I will begin with Willie, who was once my neighbor.

Willie

Willie is a natural caregiver, warm and loving and great with children. She spent her work life as a nanny and housekeeper for a variety of families, many within the music business. In her last position, one of the children Willie cared for graduated and is going off to college and one is in the process of finishing high school. She found herself not wanting to continue in this line of work, once her "kids" didn't need her anymore. All her life, Willie has loved baking. Within the last four months, she was offered to partner with someone in the music business managing an arts and crafts store. Within the partnership is the opportunity to sell home baked goods, not only within the store, but also at another store at a marina, a few miles away. This person in the music business has the discretionary funds to offer this position, but needed a warm body to breathe life into his dream while offering Willie a chance to follow her dream. Kismet!

Edith Costanza , M.Ed.

Becky

Becky is the best customer service person I know. For 30 years she worked in the commercial photographic/ graphic business. She experienced all the changes brought on by the digital revolution, and finally watched her field die. This 51 year old manager found herself unemployed with the need to reinvent herself. Her task was to figure out her skill set and extrapolate what could transfer. In Becky's case, she focused on her customer service skills. Through networking with an acquaintance, Becky heard about an exciting job at a local non-profit agency. This agency is dedicated to helping people from various cultures transition into this culture and find housing and jobs. Becky interviewed for the position and wrote a "thank you" email to the person who had given her the job lead. She expressed her excitement at the possibility of being instrumental in helping people of another culture transition into this one.

Though Becky was not hired for this job, her "thank you" email impressed the acquaintance. Shortly thereafter, the acquaintance needed someone at her agency part-time to answer the phone. It also happened that another position was vacant around this time. Because Becky was doing such good work on the phones, and co-workers could see what an asset she would be to the workplace, she was offered a full-time position.

Edith Costanza, M.Ed.

Nine years later, under the title of "Lending Associate", Becky has become an expert in her field. She continues to work for this particular non-profit organization that administers funds to Davidson County and surrounding areas that are earmarked or designed for affordable housing. Her work has been instrumental in providing flood relief and now she is part of a new program to help people address foreclosure issues. Becky's desire to help people and to be of service is manifested daily in the work she offers to our community.

Jerry

Jerry is a 60 year old male and former vice-president in the publishing world. To quote his experience:

"Thirty years in the same industry and what happens at the end. Nothing? No, something incredibly different as it turns out for me. It wasn't the first time I'd been laid off, but it was a critical time.

The magazine industry had been very good to me, I worked hard, spent probably too much time away from my family, but was successful. Just comfortable, no more. The career started at 27 and ended at 57. This was a financial consideration for them. The company was barely making money and when you consider the key operations and IT people versus a sales and customer service guy, the sales guy gets laid off first. I didn't try to find a job, never even put together a résumé. What do you do at 57, especially in this economy?

A couple of months later I met a friend who suggested that I do volunteer work, just to get out of the house and do something! I started volunteering at a local non-profit, beginning in January 2009. I walked into a world that simply blew me away. After a few months, the 3 days a week as a volunteer morphed into a full-time job. It felt good, going home every day with a smile on my face, feeling that I'd accomplished more than I ever did in my previous career. I can't describe the feeling working with our participants as closely as I have for nearly 3 years now. Simple things, like sending a fax, are important to them. Lending an ear is also important, sometimes offering advice. Never having been in recovery or imprisoned I had to learn to understand some of their individual situations, so it's emotionally challenging for me. I wasn't trained for this and I had no knowledge of this part of the world. But what a great change, one that's provided a totally new perspective of life."

Edith

Edith, the author of this guide, graduated from the Peabody College Human Resource Development Master's program in 1989. Over the next twenty years as an independent consultant, she specialized in Diversity Training through an internationally known organization, and worked in career outplacement services with two nationally recognized organizations.

Concurrently, she pursued her dreams of acting and making art. Eleven years ago, she took a full-time position as a training and development specialist with a local training academy. She had hoped to retire from this job. Fifteen months later the academy was dissolved due to governmental budget cuts. Through networking, a friend told her that a particular organization was looking for someone with a training background who was also an artist, and who had knowledge in the field of addictions, which she had.

Now, as art therapist for this organization, she works with people whose self-confidence has been battered. Completing art projects in a variety of mediums instills a sense of competence and accomplishment in her students. She is scheduled at the organization one day a week. The rest of the time, she makes art, auditions for film and commercial work, gives workshops based on her one woman show, "Snapshots From the Road," or contracts out to organizations writing various types of instructional materials.

Now into her tenth year at the organization, she credits it as the impetus for her evolving growth and creativity in all types of artistic expression.

Edith Costanza, M.Ed.

Edith Costanza, M.Ed.

R10

Rejoice

Edith Costanza, M.Ed.

Edith Costanza , M.Ed.

R10: Rejoice

Be content with what you have;
rejoice in the way things are;
when you realize there is nothing lacking,
the whole world belongs to you.

– Lao Tsu

Edith Costanza, M.Ed.

Now it is time to look back and notice how far you have come on your journey

You began by gathering your spiritual, emotional, intellectual, and physical resources. You devoted the time necessary to reflect upon your life and identified your set of skills and qualities.

Next, you explored how those skills and qualities could transfer into similar work or be built into something new as you brainstormed, researched, and wrote about yourself. You opened yourself to the possibility of alternative types of work and lifestyle. You placed yourself on a daily schedule that incorporated personal time and provided you with ways to stay refreshed and positive.

You read about others who successfully walked the road you are on and were able to regroup from job loss. Finally, you have gone the distance and can look back.

I hope you are able to absorb the blessings offered you from this loss and that you feel more equipped and confident as you move forward.

I wish you all the best.   I wish you well.

Edith Costanza, M.Ed.

Edith Costanza, M.Ed.

*For more information
about the author,
follow her blog and website.*

EdithCostanza.wordpress.com

www.EdithCostanza.com

Edith Costanza, M.Ed.